Relax
with...
Watercolour

Watercolour Painting...
Made Easy

by acclaimed Painter
and TV presenter
Harry Feeney

Design: Artefact Ltd.,

Photography: Neill Warner, Galway

Distribution by:
    Relax with Watercolour,
    The Foxford Lodge,
    Pontoon Road,
    Foxford, Co. Mayo.
    Telephone: +353 (0)94 9257777
    Website: relaxwithwatercolour.com

ISBN 97809560495-0-6

Printed in Ireland by Future Print Ltd.

To my Family …

CONTENTS

INTRODUCTION

" MAKE THE DECISION TO PAINT ... "

PLEASE READ THIS ...

If you were planning on becoming an actor, it's no good going to see the finished production ... what could you learn?

It's the rehearsals that should interest you, how the polished finished acts came into being.

If you wanted to learn a foreign language you would be expected to imitate sounds and repeat words and phrases until you were blue in the face! This is done so that this repetition sinks in so you can recall these words and phrases as you wish to use them.

As with the actor and rehearsals imitation is one of the keys to success, the language student relies on repetition to learn the language, both of these apply equally well when learning to paint.

Practice ... no matter what the task you are hoping to achieve you will always do it better when you practice and keep practicing ... I still have to and I'm painting for years. I don't know it all, I never will but I am always a willing student, always trying new ideas and ways to improve the way I paint. Make the techniques your own, put your own stamp on them.

What makes a good painter? It's very simple really, now all of you have this secret contained within the book. So don't tell a soul, let them discover the secret themselves.

Observation ... that's it, that's the key, when you learn to look and look to learn you will become a good painter. It's no big secret at all, but one day the penny will drop and then you will begin to enjoy your painting more.

It's worth reading again "learn to look" and "look to learn" try this

LEARN TO LOOK AND READ THE

THE BOOK

Well, did you see it? If you didn't, read it again … keep reading it until that penny drops! So how do you learn to look? By studying shapes, lines and colour you can achieve distance, focus on detail and make colour choice second nature. So now you know, no magic wands, no short cuts and no quick fix remedies, just plain old fashioned hard work and those two words again

Practice and Observation.

Drawing is one of the finest ways of educating the eye because it involves a concentrated exercise in seeing and heightening visual awareness.

Forget for the moment of trying to draw and paint pretty pictures but try as much as you can to do an investigative study of an everyday item. One of my favourites is a shoe lace. Hold the lace in one hand and let it drop and whatever way it lands. Try and draw it, see how it overlaps loops and all of that. This is one of the best exercises to do and it costs nothing but your time. The amount of knowledge you will learn is amazing ... give it a go.

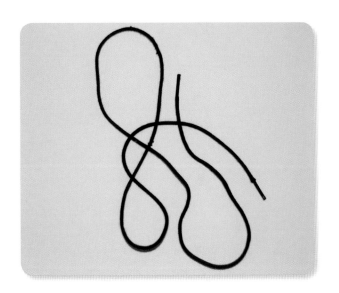

Learn to re-develop your curiosity. When you were an infant you would have stared and studied everything for a long time, curiosity will give you fresh eyes.

A LITTLE HISTORY

Harry Feeney was born in Derry during the mid fifties, the family had squatted into a Nissan Hut in a disused American naval base called "Springtown Camp" as there was a serious housing problem in the city.

Eventually the family was housed in the Brandywell area, an area of extremely high unemployment. Money was scarce and food wasn't much better but there was an amazing community spirit. He grew up through the troubles and witnessed many incidents that a young man should only read or see as a fiction story on the big screen. He decided in the mid seventies that if he didn't get away he would end up in jail or dead. Neither of these options appealed naturally, so Harry took a huge risk and set off from Derry's ... Strabane Old Road, he stuck his thumb out and took a lift from a passing motorist who was travelling to Dublin.

Many years earlier a teacher considered his artistic attempts as an insult to the teacher's intelligence. Such was the time we lived in that a single comment like that would be enough to stop him from painting.

Taking the teacher at his word, Harry felt the teacher must be right so he stopped and subdued any further thoughts of painting or drawing for over 20 years. These feelings persisted and eventually came to the fore. Harry began to paint, and it must be said with the help of a lesson with Frank Clarke, suddenly pieces of the jigsaw began to slot into place. Harry then started to excel and found a new lease of life, and his appetite for painting grew and grew. Books were not enough and after sometime following mistake after mistake he began to realise that he wasn't making mistakes at all but he was making discoveries. Just like Harry, the word mistake began a new lease of life; both of them became discoveries. He began painting seriously in 1990

and by 1995 he gave up the day job and began painting for a living which he has continued to do successfully to this day.

RELAX WITH WATERCOLOUR (THE STARTER)

Welcome to the first book from the series "Relax with Watercolour", known as "The Starter" … if we get to another book it is going to be known as "The Main Course".

This book is designed to put you at ease and to help remove those obstacles that I often hear such as "I have a fear of watercolour", "it's too difficult", or "It gets all muddy on me", " I tried it and it went wrong, anyway I prefer oils or acrylics it's easier" … etc., etc. It's all true, and the only thing that qualifies me to write this book is the fact that I have done all of the above and got it wrong many times too!

But getting it wrong so many times and each time learning a little bit more helped me to get better. Gradually I did get better and the more I painted

the fewer mistakes I made but I also learned to call my mistakes discoveries, as I discovered something new every time I got it wrong.

This was a major breakthrough for me as I turned around my amateur unguided scribbles and attempts into a real confidence booster and actually just painted this and that to see what would happen.

So in order to help you I have written a step by step guide for the different projects from my discoveries.

Most people starting to paint for the first time have that fear of people laughing that them or making themselves look foolish as they have no idea where to start or how for that matter.

This is soon overcome when you can make that decision to paint, this is a huge step as it wipes away the fear of "the thought" … That's the thought in your mind of "you can't paint, so don't bother".

This is a very real thought and one that needs to be addressed before you can even think of painting. I took command of my lack of painting confidence and did one simple thing, I made this decision to just have a go, to try it.

Once you decide, that's it! It gets easier and your determination to succeed will grow. The second thing is encouragement, from a loved one, friend or family, this is inspiring when people are right behind you and not laughing at you, let's face it to make an effort under duress is a major achievement in itself. The most important part of this whole process is … **MAKE THE DECISION TO PAINT**.

To learn my watercolour technique you have to first understand what is going to happen next then apply it. This is the most important piece of advice and is the key to success … know what is going to happen next. If you were learning to drive you wouldn't drive away without tuition. Painting is no different. So with the help of this book and the DVD's, I'm confident that I can get you on the right road before you drive away!

Each project is fully self contained and explained in simple steps so that you can enjoy the benefits of the book and learn the techniques.

All I ask is that for you to become competent is that you do three things …

Practice, make mistakes, make discoveries.

The relax with watercolour brush set, which consists of 6 brushes.

The new redesigned Hake, with the shorter handle for a more balanced and comfortable hold.

The Trees, Shrubs and Foliage Brushes x 2.... These brushes would be more at home with oils or acrylics but I have found them invaluable as you can create all the various foliage shapes quite easily with these brushes.

Fine Detail Brushes … 3 of the finest sable brushes to capture detail.

The number 6 and 4 will achieve much of your detail work and the rigger for masts of boats, reeds and twigs and branches.

I will recommend other brushes as you progress and improve.

Watercolour paper 140 lb rough is my paper of choice but you can experiment and use what suits your style.

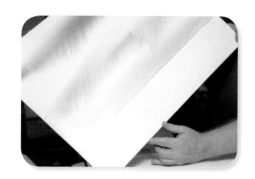

Winsor & Newton Cotman range of paints and my basic palette of 8 colours is as follows: ultramarine blue, yellow ochre, burnt sienna, burnt umber, indigo, sap green, lemon yellow and alizarin crimson.

My auxiliary colours that I dip into as required are raw umber, light red, neutral tint, cerulean blue, Prussian blue, mauve, cadmium yellow (artist range), viridian olive green and very occasionally titanium white (acrylic).

2 pots of water (one for applying water to the paper and the other is to clean the brushes). Keep them separate as you will forget. On several occasions I have dipped my brush into a cup of tea!

A good, big palette to mix colours. I use an old door panel from a UPVC door, it's a fantastic palette and it was destined for the dump before I met it ... but now it lives happily in my studio. It's always a good thing to have plenty of

tissues or kitchen roll and baby wipes are great, though a few of your neighbours might start to think you are getting ready for a big event ... and if you haven't painted before then it is, maybe not the big event they had in mind!

PREPARATION

Getting ready to paint is very important, have everything in its place before you begin. Start with your chosen sky colours only on your palette. I say this because so many people put out all the colours they have and end up scraping paint into the bin, so just put out what you need and only when you need it.

Brushes ready, chamois if you have one to absorb water or an old cloth. Paint the painting in your mind first before you start, just an idea of where things are going.

If you are right handed then put the equipment on your right side, I have witnessed many people stretching across their painting to reach for this and that then get annoyed with themselves for being silly when it falls on their painting.

This preparation will begin to rise your expectations and that fear of failure will now begin to kick in. This is a very critical time for you. It's here where you decide whether you take charge and make an effort however it turns out or do you leave the paper blank? Remember it's only a piece of paper!

Whatever mark you make will be groundbreaking so enjoy, be courageous and remember that **"courage is fear that has said its prayers"**.

As much as is physically possible, try not to touch the paper with your fingers as they leave the natural oils from your hand on the paper and you get a greasy residue that the paint skips over just like it would a waxy crayon.

PAINTING EXERCISES

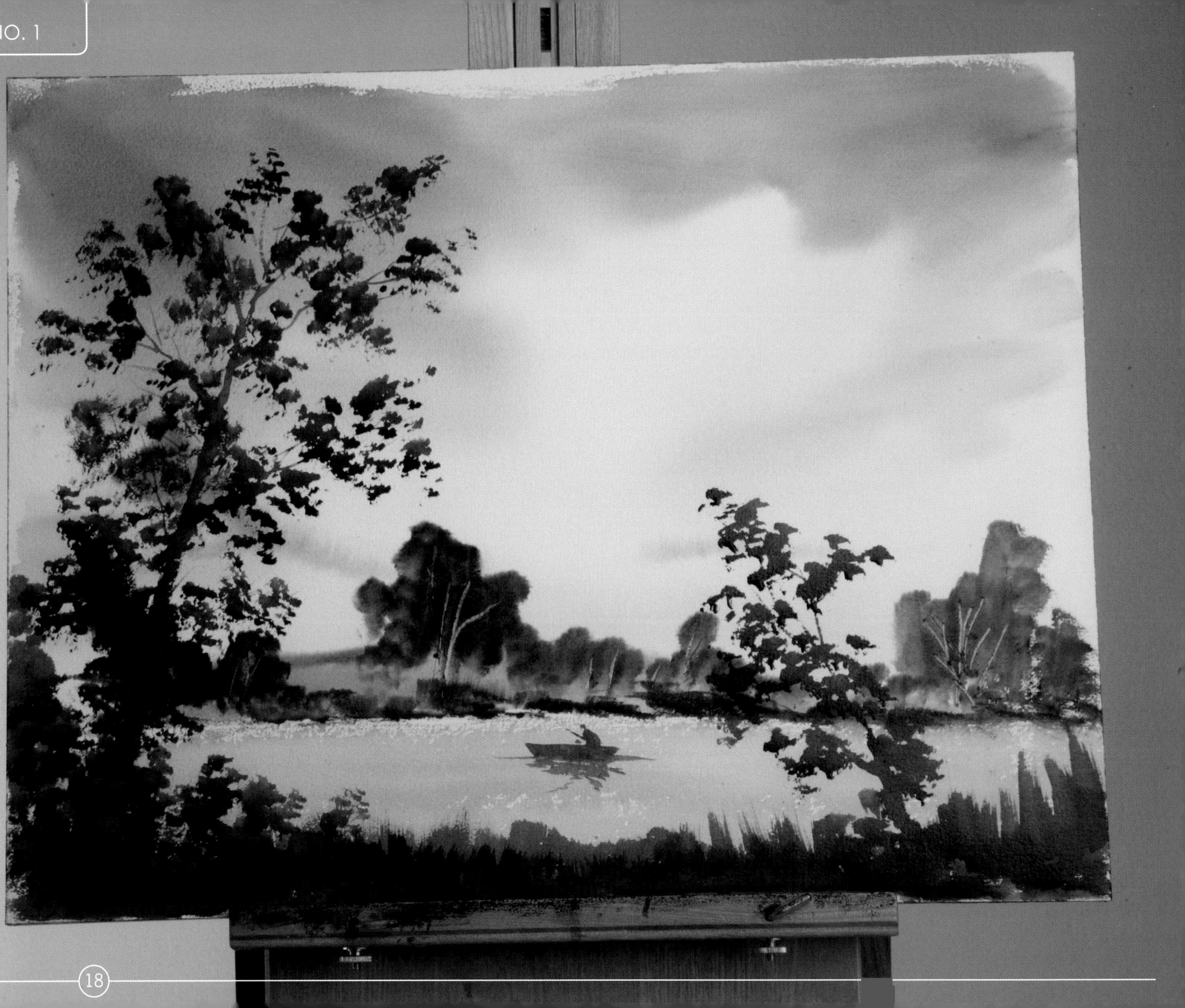

"LOUGH CONN" MONOCHROME PAINTING (ONE COLOUR)

This painting will get you on the right road to better watercolour. The one colour is the best way to understand tone, the further away something is the lighter the tone and the nearer you bring it the darker the tone. Lough Conn is one of the great limestone loughs in the west of Ireland.

PAINTING STAGES OVERVIEW

STEP 1.

PREPARATION
Flood the paper with water. Relax, get to know the brush and find a way it fits your hand best

STEP 4.

SPARKLING WATER
How to create sparkling water through speed of delivery

STEP 2.

THE SKY
This is where the water colour show begins. Apply the colour and witness the magic

STEP 5.

FOREGROUND
Observe the colour tones building up in the foreground

STEP 3.

MIDDLEGROUND
Add distance and dimension using light and dark tones contrast

STEP 6.

ADDING DETAIL
Use specific detail brushes for adding detailed finishing touches

REQUIRED MATERIALS

- A set of relax with watercolour brushes
- A tube of W & N indigo paint
- Arches aquarelle 140 lb rough block
- 2 jars of water, damp rag and your time

STEP 1 – PREPARATION

This is your launch pad to better painting, we start with one colour and for this painting we will use indigo, a sort of blue/grey colour, that shows great light when contrasted against the natural white of the paper. Remember here that less is more. Use the colour sparingly.

As is the "Relax with Watercolour" way and what has become our signature and as we do in all our paintings, we start by flooding water into the top ⅔ of the paper. Use the Hake brush for this, make sure you use plenty of water as it won't harm the paper. Use your brush to create a horizon line, (see photo 1) it doesn't have to be straight on this painting so don't get caught up trying to level it up. When you feel it's wet enough, wet it again.

Keep your paper on the flat for the moment, otherwise the water will just flow away too fast.

STEP 2 – THE SKY

Remember now that your paper is wet so you don't need to wet the paint … the brush should hold enough water to keep an neat edge on it. If it's too wet it won't work well. Tease the brush into the paint, don't plunge the brush into it. We don't want clots of pigment stuck on the brush, so mix it well on the palette first and not on the painting. Just a quick swipe across (see photo 1.2). Discipline yourself here as we need plenty of white paper here to reflect the light. Try and keep the centre of the paper clear of all brush strokes and colour. (see photo 1.2a) GET THE BRUSH OUT OF YOUR HAND. Now let's rock and roll. Move and tilt the paper to disperse the colour (see photo 1.2b).

Enjoy this, it's not often you get to watch paint dry! The more opportunities you get to do this the better you will become at it. Now go back into heavier paint this time as we want to create the illusion of depth (see photo 1.2c). Again we rock and roll to allow the colours to blend. Once you're happy with the sky leave the painting flat to dry and settle into the paper.

📷 1.3

STEP 3 – MIDDLEGROUND

Your painting needs to be completely dry now before you can continue.

Keeping with the Hake brush, load the brush again with colour, make it fairly wet this time as you are now going to paint on dry paper (see photo 1.3). Hold the brush at about 30 degrees to the horizon and sweep across creating the lay of the land (see photo 1.3a).

Keep the brush moving until you reach the other side and then, with horizontal strokes, pull the paint down to achieve a nice level line that will become your water level (see photo 1.3b).

We now add in darker tones creating tree shapes with our tree brush (see photo 1.3c). Continue along putting in trees here and there (see photo 1.3d).

1.4

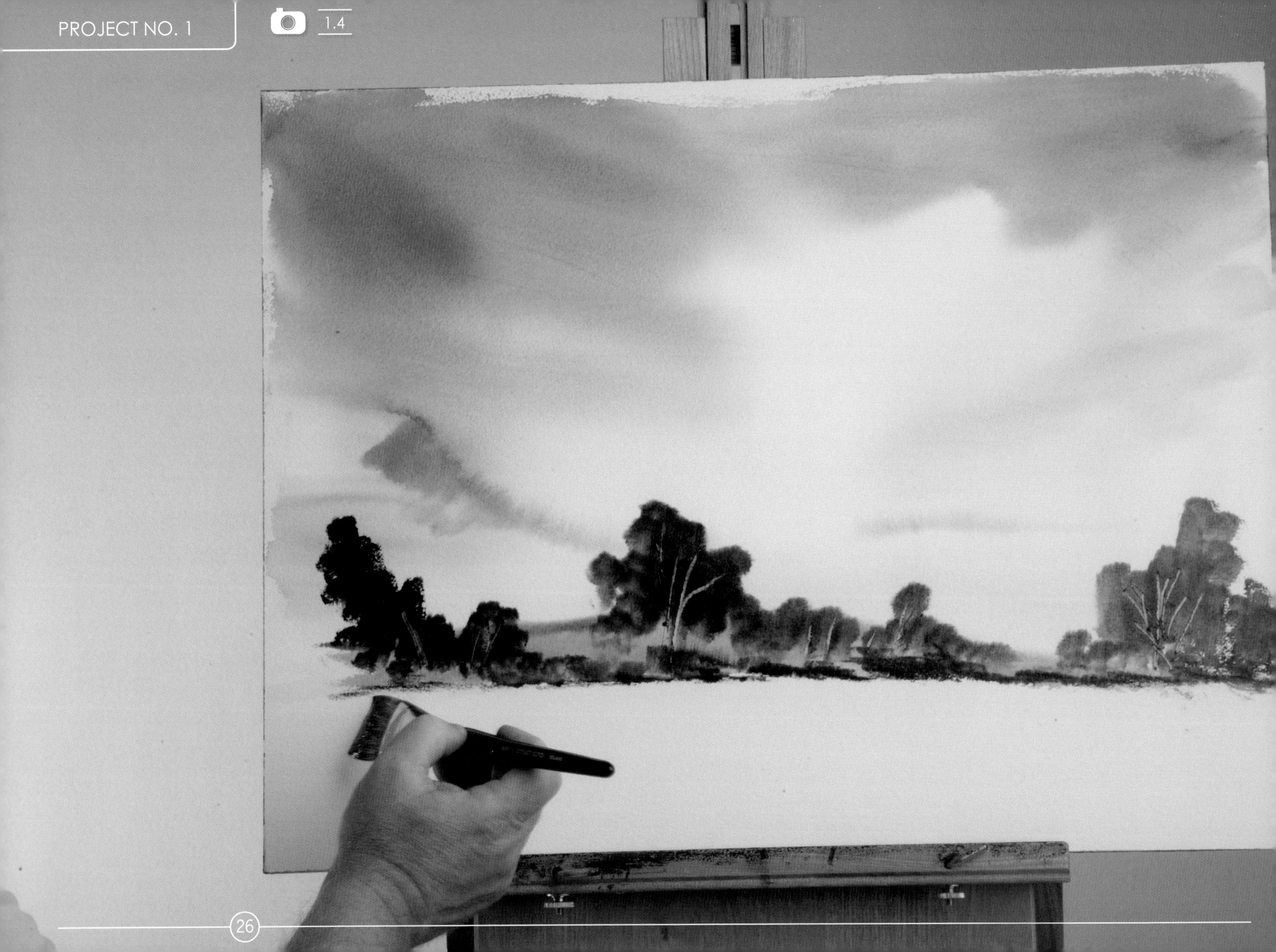

STEP 4 – SPARKLING WATER

Take the hake brush again (see photo 1.4) and this time we are going to capture the sparkle on water, to do this speed is essential, don't hold back on this.

Just go for it (see photo 1.4a, 1.4b). Keep the brush stroke going in one direction only, do not come back on the brush stroke otherwise you'll loose the sparkle (see photo 1.4c).

STEP 5 – FOREGROUND

Everything must be dry now to proceed. You can use a dryer or, as I do when I'm not in any rush, let it dry naturally, it does make a difference. Using the flat tree brush and thick paint we now put in the foreground (see photo 1.5, 1.5a, 1.5b), very little water is used at this stage, tap the brush through to pick up the paint.

Let's add in a couple of trees, keep using the flat tree brush for this to create the tree trunk (see photo 1.5c).

Add in branches using the rigger brush (see photo 1.5d). Now we can add some foliage using the flat tree brush again (see photo 1.5e). Stand back take a look, make sure it looks like a tree and foliage. We'll add in another tree now to give balance to the painting (see photo 1.5f).

STEP 6 – ADDING DETAIL

Time for finishing touches so let's add in a little boatman. Using the small detail brush first we paint a small rectangle then add 2 small triangles, one each end of the rectangle. Now centre the brush on the rectangle and simply touch the paper with the small detail brush (see photo 1.6).

Finishing off with a fishing rod (see photo 1.6a) then finally reflect all this into the water in the following sequence (see photo 1.6b) ... and this is how the finished painting will look like. Sign and admire.

Well that's that and well done. E-mail me your attempt, I'd love to see it and have it on our relax gallery. The more you paint this scene the better you will become. Remember you can literally move mountains when your painting sometimes; have the mountains to the right, another day to the left, experiment. I guarantee each time it will be different!

"LOVERS IN THE MIST"

This painting gives you an opportunity to use many colours without getting them muddy and it's simple to do. Only add in 3 or 5 birds as it is more appealing to the eye.

PAINTING STAGES OVERVIEW

PREPARATION
This painting will require you to flood the whole page

REQUIRED MATERIALS

- Lemon yellow, alizarin crimson and yellow ochre
- The hake brush, large detail brush and rigger
- 2 pots of water, damp rag
- No drawing required

THE SKY
Add the 3 colours consecutively and watch them blending into a warm, sunrise scene

ADDING DETAIL
Use small brush. Practice making bird shapes always placing an odd number of them

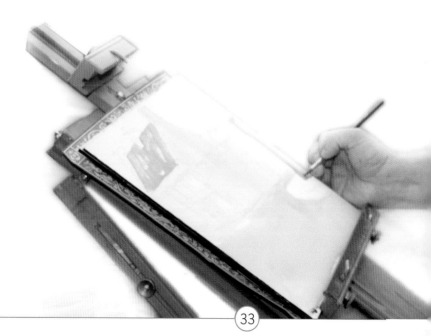

STEP 1 – BACKGROUND PREPARATION

As before, flood the paper only this time no horizon line, just cover all the paper with water (see photo 2.1).

Apply the colours as written (lemon yellow, yellow ochre, alizarin crimson), do not clean the brush between colours just keep applying as they are getting darker with each application. So first colour to use is lemon yellow (see photo 2.1a - 2.1b), straight into yellow ochre then apply alizarin, then let it all dry totally.

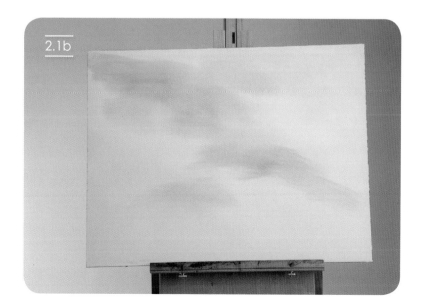

STEP 2 – FINE DETAIL

We then paint in 2 figures with the weak mixture of ultramarine blue and alizarin crimson to give the illusion of mist (see photo 2.2, 2.2a).

Create a shadow by dragging the brush from the figures to one side (see photo 2.2b).

STEP 3 – FINISHING TOUCHES

Coming to the finishing stages, you may have to practice making bird shapes for a while, particularly if you have just created a wonderful painting. I always do my birds like a plane landing and taking off, a gentle touch done then a gentle take off (see photo 2.3, 2.3a). It's important here to keep the brush moving while landing and taking off otherwise you are about to make a new discovery! Another finished painting (see photo 2.3b). Put in about 3,5 or 7 birds (never an even number), sign and admire. If you have a digital camera take a photo of it and e-mail it to us for our newsletter and gallery.

2.3a

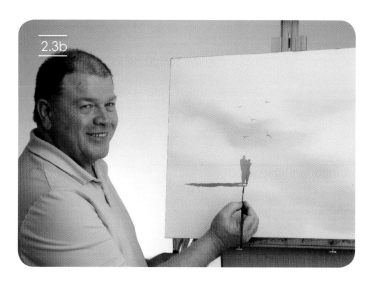

2.3b

"BOATS" DRAWING PRACTICE SESSION

This little project is very important and will enhance your drawing skills and how you visualize your paintings. The core of the drawing is the number 8 turned on it's side (see photo 3.1). Just start off by continually drawing the number 8 side on. Add the intersecting lines as you see them but be careful where you place them, it's not as easy as it looks.

People often ask me to do the boat sequence, so I have included it in the book. It's self explanatory on how it is achieved, to get good at this technique requires plenty of practice and simply study each diagram, where the lines intersect. Over time and practise you will master this to the point that you don't even have to draw the sequence anymore to get your boats perfect every time.

REQUIRED MATERIALS

A HB Pencil and a good eraser

"THE COTTAGE"

We are combining your new found drawing skills from project 3 with painting this time. Take plenty of time for this and most important enjoy it. Pay attention to the shadow areas as they show light and dimension.

PAINTING STAGES OVERVIEW

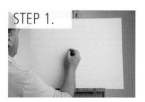

STEP 1.

DRAWING
Using a HB pencil simply follow our sequence to achieve a great sketch

STEP 4.

PAINTING THE COTTAGE
Experiment with light and shade to achieve depth within the painting

STEP 2.

THE SKY
Learn to precisely control your hake brush

STAGE 5.

ADDING DETAIL
Observe terrain landscape when you apply darker tones to the foreground

REQUIRED MATERIALS

- Start with a HB pencil and a good eraser
- The arches watercolour block
- Then add yellow ochre , burnt sienna and burnt umber and a hint of indigo
- 2 jars of water, damp rag and a set of the relax brushes

STEP 3.

THE ROOF
Develop consistent brush strokes while keeping edges clear of paint

STEP 1 – DRAWING

First we have to draw the cottage and I have broken this down into manageable pencil stroke stages, follow this to the letter and you will have great results. Remember there is no horizon, it's not needed.

First draw the side gable to the chimney (see photo 4.1, 4.1a).

Now you have to follow the sequences in order to achieve the required result, they are self explanatory (see photo 4.1b, 4.1c).

4.2

4.2a

4.2b

4.2c

STEP 2 – THE SKY

Continue the sequence right until you end up with a complete house sketch (see photo 4.2). Well done, that's an achievement in itself, now all you have to do is add some colour.

You can run a wet line across the painting outlining the house, in other words paint the water around the house. Be careful that you don't get the water in on the building otherwise it will just flood in. Take a little care here and it will pay dividends to you. If you look side-on you will see that the shiny paper is where you have wet it and the flat looking bits will be dry. Be extra careful not to disturb your line.

Let's paint in some yellow ochre now to outline the house bring the paint around the house and across the lay of the land (see photo 4.2a, 4.2b). Turn the painting upside down now to let the paint move around freely, keep that edge of the house clear of paint (see photo 4.2c). Let it all dry naturally.

STEP 3 – THE ROOF

Keeping the painting upside down it's time to paint in the roof (see photo 4.3, 4.3a). Tidy up the edges and pay attention to keeping white space down each gable.

We add in burnt sienna now, maintaining the upside down position (see photo 4.3b).

Develop the brush strokes downward towards you at the same angle as the roof. Last colour now, burnt umber is applied across the same area (see photo 4.3c). Again develop these brush strokes. Turn the painting right side up now and add in a few more delicate brush strokes to enhance the roof (see photo 4.3d, 4.3e).

Again it's important to make sure the painting is dry before continuing.

📷 4.4

4.4a

4.4b

4.4c

STEP 4 – PAINTING THE COTTAGE

Add a brush stroke of indigo to water, colouring the water but at the same time having enough to be more than a tint ... this is for your shadow areas (see photo 4.4, 4.4a).

Pull the shadow out onto the lay of the land. Carefully paint in the shadow under the thatch and add in the shadow to the reveals of the windows and doors (see photo 4.4b, 4.4c). Don't forget the inside of the chimney.

Take the yellow ochre now and swipe across the land in front of the cottage (see photo 4.4d - 4.4g).

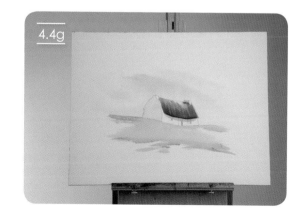

STEP 5 – ADDING FINE DETAIL

Clean the brush, then take a small detail brush and brush in the windows and door (see photo 4.5, 4.5a).

Take a mix of burnt umber and a touch of indigo to paint in a little stack of turf on the side (see photo 4.5b). Add in a few finishing touches now in the front of the painting (see photo 4.5c-4.5f). Sign and admire

E-mail us your efforts and we'll post it on our gallery.

www.relaxwithwatercolour.com

53

"DOGS BAY, CONNEMARA"

Relax with... Watercolour

This is such a fantastic location and we use several different techniques during the session. There are really 2 paintings in this if you look at it carefully, end one at the sand dunes ... below that is good enough to be another painting. So really you could do either or both or it all at the one time.

PAINTING STAGES OVERVIEW

STEP 1.

THE SKY
Combination of water, sky colours and areas of white paper (knock out)

STEP 2.

MIDDLEGROUND
Test your brush stroke again, keeping it constant across the whole page

STEP 3.

SPARKLING WATER
Advance the technique learned first on the monochrome painting

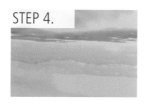

STEP 4.

SAND DUNES
Keep it uneven, just like the strong Atlantic winds would do

STAGE 5.

FOREGROUND
Discover a creative technique using just an old photo and a cloth

REQUIRED MATERIALS

- Ultramarine blue, alizarin crimson, yellow ochre, burnt sienna, burnt umber
- Arches aquarelle block
- 2 jars water, damp cloth
- An old photograph
- No drawing required

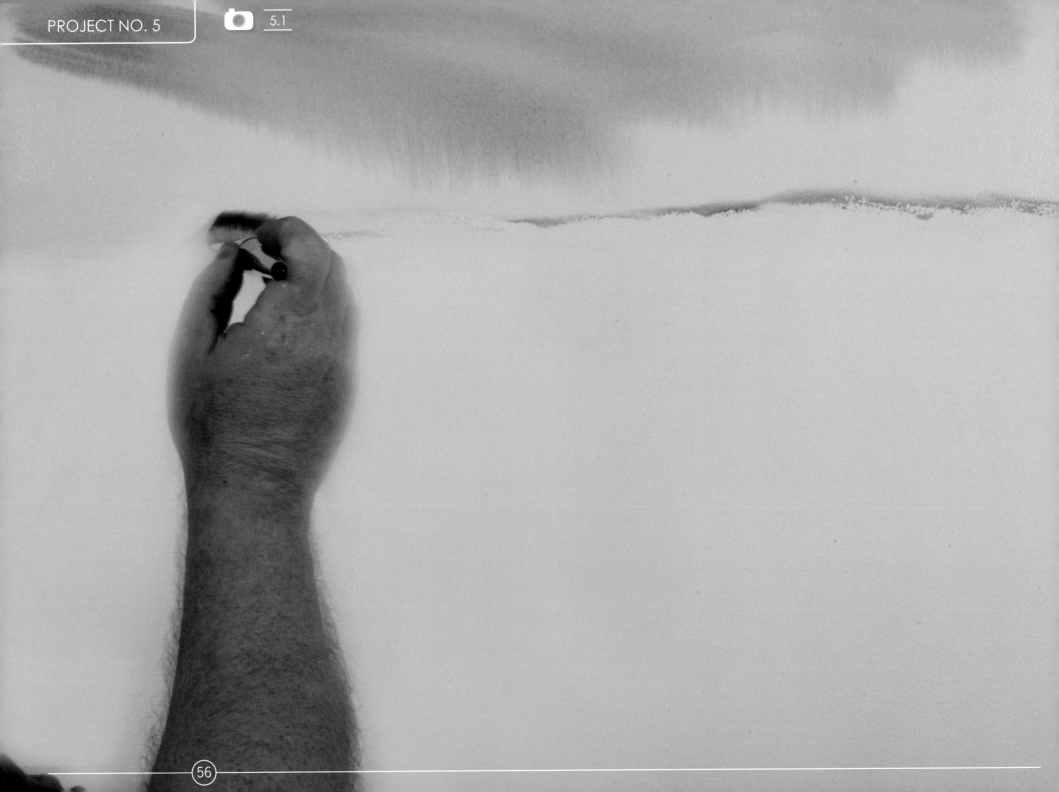

STEP 1 – THE SKY

We have no drawing to contend with so that should fill you with confidence right away. Wet your paper ⅔ of the way down, pay particular attention to the edges and use your brush to draw the horizon line. The dry edge will hold the water back as long as you don't raise your paper too much or leave it up for too long. Introduce ultramarine blue (see photo 5.1), mix it well to ensure the pigment has dispersed, then apply it leaving as much white space of the paper as you desire. Add a little alizarin crimson to the blue now to achieve a different tone for the sky.

Let's rock and roll! Move the paint around so that it covers all areas you want the paint to reach, enjoy this as it will turn out well in most cases. Remember to keep white spaces to allow the white of the paper to help illuminate the painting. Gently tilt the paper back and forward to distribute the paint on the paper evenly and then rest it to allow the paint soak into the paper.

STEP 2 – MIDDLEGROUND

We now have the distant mountains of Clare to consider which is one side of Galway bay. Using a mixture of the sky colours again, ultramarine blue and alizarin (see photo 5.2, 5.2a).

Mix them both leaning on the side of the blue, in other words we don't want a reddish type colour. Gently angle your hake to lean into the mountains, move your brush across, remembering not to stop or lift the brush, keep the brush stroke even and constant until you reach the far end of the paper.

Finish off by evening out the bottom of the mountain (see photo 5.2b) to create the water surface lapping against the bottom of the cliffs. Again this must dry before moving on to the next step.

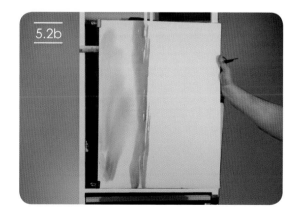

STEP 3 – ADDING THE SPARKLE

We are still on the same 2 colours to create the open water in Galway bay. First we get our mix right and the next technique is straight forward; you just sweep the brush across the paper in a even line. The only, but most important difference here, is the speed. You must do this very fast to achieve the broken sparkle of the water (see photo 5.3). As before you must dry this stage before continuing.

STEP 4 – SAND DUNES

Now we have to get in the sand dunes, creating dogs bay ... see how much we have achieved with just 2 colours. Let's introduce another couple of colours to the palette. Yellow ochre and burnt sienna. Apply the yellow ochre first in a broken uneven style creating the lay of the land and the sand dunes (see photo 5.4). Introduce the burnt sienna here and there to create shadows and depth (see photo 5.4a - 5.4c). We need to swipe across some more sparkling water effects here but this time swipe from right to left so that the broken sparkle effect laps up on the shore (see photo 5.4d).

Moving along make sure again that each stage is dry ... almost finished now.

5.5

5.5a

5.5b

5.5c

STEP 5 – FOREGROUND

So onto the foreground and darker colours to give the illusion of foreground ... burnt umber and a hint of indigo. Sweeping in here and there making reeds, grasses and bogland. Some side swipes with the number 6 detail brush creating walls and a few posts receding into the water ... any posts in the water reflect them into the water (see photo 5.5).

A few reeds and dark foliage in one corner and almost finished. Now take an old photograph ... cut out a long triangular shape (see photo 5.5a) place on the painting where you would like to see a boat, then rub gently but firmly over the cut out with a baby wipe and remove the paint (see photo 5.5b, 5.5c) Gently lift the photograph and dry. A dark brush stroke across the bottom of the boat and your done (see photo 5.5d). Sign and admire.

5.5d

"ROCKS"

People are wary of rocks and how to paint them. In this exercise I will show you how to have success with the rock technique. Don't forget to add the boat at the end.

PAINTING STAGES OVERVIEW

STEP 1.

THE SKY
Use plenty of water for our colours to float in

STEP 3.

THE ROCKS
Build up colour gradually, enhancing rock proportions

STEP 2.

THE MIDDLEGROUND
By now you're probably a pro at creating sparkling water effect

STAGE 4.

ADDING DETAIL
Learn a new usage for your credit card (without spending a penny)

REQUIRED MATERIALS

- Ultramarine blue, light red, yellow ochre
- Arches aquarelle block
- 2 jars water, damp cloth
- Credit or other plastic card
- No drawing required

STEP 1 – THE SKY

Wet the sky as before ⅔ of the way down, plenty of water as we have to float in the colours, apply yellow ochre to the horizon and just above (see photo 6.1). Swipe a weak solution of light red, followed by the ultramarine blue. (see photo 6.1a).

Let the sky dry completely before proceeding the next stage.

6.1a

STEP 2 – THE MIDDLEGROUND

Take the mix of ultramarine blue and light red, a slightly tinted mauve or violet colour is the desired effect, make sure it's very wet before applying. Swipe across very fast to get the sparkle of your sea (see photo 6.2, 6.2a). Let it dry.

6.2a

6.3a

6.3b

STEP 3 – THE ROCKS

Now we are ready to start putting in our rocks. Start in the distance. Light tones required here and it's important to start light. As we paint towards the bottom of the page, we creep nearer and nearer to the viewer, namely you or your audience … at each stage you add a little more colour increasing the tone (see photo 6.3 - 6.3b). Another thing that happens as you increase the tone, is you also make your "rocks" bigger. Imagine you had a magnifying glass … as you slowly bring it to your eye everything increases in size.

As you push it way everything recedes. So it is here with the rocks, you can judge it yourself, though remember to start small otherwise you will have Mount Everest beside you as you increase the sizes.

The foreground is also rocks and more rocks, use your imagination here and create your own style rocks (see photo 6.3c, 6.3d).

STEP 4 – FINE DETAIL

Just to add a focal point into the painting I have included a boat and mast. … Start off with the credit card and push it through dark paint to moisten the edge. (see photo 6.4).

Apply in a vertical direction (that's straight up and down) about 4 inches long, start drawing the boat shape to your satisfaction, (see photo 6.4a). Reflect it all into the water (see photo 6.4b) and don't complicate it by trying to paint an upside down replica … KEEP IT SIMPLE

Stand back, have a look. Sign and Admire.

6.4a

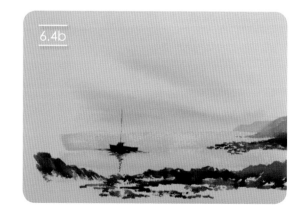

6.4b

www.relaxwithwatercolour.com

HARRY'S HELPFUL HINTS

HARRY'S HELPFUL HINTS

Make a number of studies of each step until you are familiar with the subject … you will amaze yourself.

Trees – before attempting a tree in full foliage, draw a single leaf first, then a cluster, now a branch, now a few branches then finally the full tree.

Shadows – should always be drawn very carefully as they provide clues to shapes and are very useful for composition aids in any painting.

Skies leaving gaps or holes in the sky – will give the impression of clouds so don't try to fill every inch of sky area with paint. Always paint the sky to the horizon and not the top of the mountains … mountains go over your sky not under it. We need to make the impression of the sky dipping behind the mountain.

Folds – like you would find in a garment or tablecloths etc. , they help define form or shape and give dimension to a drawing or painting.

Light – this is one of the most important elements in painting, as it governs shadows and illuminates objects or a passage in a painting.

Geometrical shapes – all objects, no matter what has an underlying geometrical shape, rectangular, square, round, cylindrical or cube. So make it one of your first objectives, to get the proper shape. Then you can add a shadow which creates light and that's how to do it, so suddenly you have a complete painting.

Figure Drawing – the ability to draw figures convincingly only comes about through practise. The biggest problem will more than likely be proportion. Don't expect to get your drawings right first time, you may have to do the

Relax with...
Watercolour

same sketch many times maybe as much as 30 times before you start to see a likeness a " true likeness". Don't throw out your attempts keep these efforts and leave them aside for a day or so then look through them again, sometimes we don't see a good image staring us in the face.

Detail Drawing – this involves taking a small area of say a leaf and drawing it with as much detail as possible over a period of an hour or so. And you have to spend the hour at it, no good saying he leaf is too small. I guarantee that if you spend the time, you'll see it differently. No good trying this on something too big, as it will inevitably try your patience ... keep to a small item, even the shoe lace again. You don't have to spend the hour at one sitting, break it up into 5 or 10 minute intervals but maintain the hour. Use a HB pencil.

Painting outdoors – it is wise to accept that an outing to paint will take at least 3 to 4 hours, it's something that is better when it is planned. Allow to give

yourself a break such as lunch, don't rush and never let yourself get cold, thirsty, hungry or tired. You cannot concentrate when your body is trying to tell you one thing and you want to do another.

So plan the trip by the following:

- Allocate plenty of time to get there
- Check the weather, have a purpose when you are there
- Get into a sheltered area and protect yourself, as well as your painting (one thing that will upset most days is the wind, blowing all sorts of debris on your painting such as leaves, flies, bits of twigs)

Enjoyment Sketch – a drawing or quick painting worked on location done simply in line form simply to enjoy the experience.

Information Sketch – a drawing or painting done solely to collect information or detail to be used later at home or in the studio. Remember the leaf?

Atmosphere Sketch – a drawing to try and capture mood in a subject like movement, the wind, rain or a ray of sunlight.

Specific Sketch – this is really a combination of the information and atmosphere sketches, but the only difference is that the objective is to go to a specific place to record or capture what you can see and feel, then to use this for a larger studio painting. Remember too that finished sketches can be used as "finished works of art".

Colours for the different seasons

Spring greens – colours are clear and light, plenty of yellow for new sunlight your blues should be fresh looking, greens crisp like a mix of viridian and a

touch of white make a lovely light green. Cadmium yellow and winsor blue will give a variety of nice bright greens for those springtime trees and grasses, especially if your trying to capture the foliage in bright sunlight.

Summer greens – again the mixes of cadmium yellow and winsor will give you most tones needed for summer, but lean on the side of the yellow and add a little touch of gouache white to lift the tone.

Autumn Grass and Trees – yellow ochre is the ideal yellow to mix with ultramarine blue to give a good autumn grass colour but using yellow ochre just with a slight hint of the blue will be sufficient. You can use this for foliage too. Burnt sienna with a touch of ultramarine blue is also great for trees too, again keep the colour leaning to the sienna colour.

Thatch roofs – yellow ochre first, add in a touch of burnt sienna and finally burnt umber to enhance the shadow ... see more on this in project 3.

Winter trees – the old faithful burnt umber is a great colour and has many uses mixed with ultramarine blue for trees, branches and twigs. It can also be used for very dark late summer foliage.

Willow trees and chestnuts – in full summer they are a bluish-green so cadmium yellow and ultramarine again come into their own.

Grey skies – again we are using burnt umber and ultramarine, which gives an excellent grey colour for cloudy skies, you can also use this colour for mud flats on an estuary.

Middle Distance – light red is one of those colours that you need to be careful of so use it sparingly, mixed with the old reliable ultramarine blue will give you a nice warm grey for middle distant trees, woods or hills.

Distance – light red again but use cobalt blue or cerulean this time for distant trees and mountains. You can also use this mix for snow shadows.

Stone Walls – once more you can use the light red and cobalt blue for this and there are so many varied mixes but if you need it warmed up add yellow ochre as a wash over it to warm it up.

Brick Walls – yellow ochre mixed with alizarin crimson make a good brick colour and it can be used for tiles on a roof.

Perspective and the third dimension – is used in a painting to create the illusion of space, volume and distance involving complicated mathematics, that's the technical scientific explanation. We ordinary people who paint just call it creating depth. The first two being the length and width of your paper.

Colours – the **primary colours** or the first order of colour unmixed are BLUE, RED and YELLOW. All other colours come from these. **Secondary Colours** are made from mixing two primaries ... and they are ORANGE (mix red & yellow) GREEN (mix blue & yellow) and VIOLET (mix blue and red).

These are followed by **tertiary colours** which is a mix of primaries and secondaries. All sorts of combinations will appear here for example the colour red (primary) mixed with green (secondary) will give you brown and so on.

Primary, Secondary and Tertiary Colours Wheel and Star

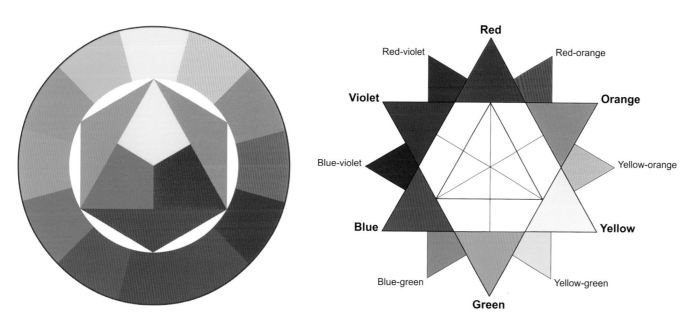

Additive mixing of primaries (pigment)

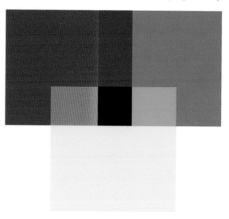

Three dimensions of colour

1. **Hue:** the common name of the colour, can be any on the colour wheel/star.

2. **Tone:** depth of the colour - lightness or darkness (light, middle or dark).

3. **Intensity:** brightness or dullness – the strength and brilliance of a colour (bright, middle intensity or dull.

Additive mixing of primaries (light)

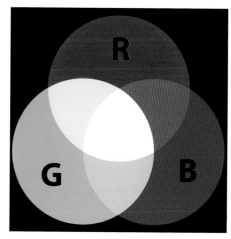

THE EPILOGUE

FINALLY – A CLOSING WORD

I hope you enjoy trying the various projects and remember Rome wasn't built in a day. If you feel that this is too daunting on your own then why don't you come to one of my workshops and I'll teach you there and then. A wise man once told me that a teacher is better than 2 books … you can't ask a book a question but having said that my website address is on the bottom of each page so if you have a question just log on and simply email me.

My DVD's and other items are for sale on my website, my workshops are located in several venues around the country, hope you can make one of them sometime or come to The Foxford Lodge for a painting Holiday.

I deliberately haven't gone into too much detail with the other bits and pieces associated with painting, as I am only featuring 'as seen on TV'.

Watercolour

These projects are quite enough on their own to contend with. Once you learn these projects you can continue your journey in the 2nd book "Relax with Watercolour " ... "The main course" bringing you to a new level.

Best of luck!

Harry